GROWING A
PERMACULTURE
FOOD
FOREST

Caleb Warnock

FAMILIUS

Copyright © 2017 by Caleb Warnock and Kami Telford
All rights reserved.

Published by Familius LLC, www.familius.com

Familius books are available at special discounts for bulk purchases, whether for sales promotions or for family or corporate use. For more information, contact Familius Sales at 559-876-2170 or email orders@familius.com.

Library of Congress Cataloging-in-Publication Data
2017942637

Print ISBN 9781945547331

Printed in the United States of America

Edited by Lindsay Sandberg
Cover design by David Miles
Book design by Maggie Wickes

10 9 8 7 6 5 4 3 2 1

First Edition

GROWING A
PERMACULTURE
FOOD
FOREST

HOW TO CREATE
A GARDEN ECOSYSTEM
YOU ONLY PLANT ONCE
BUT CAN HARVEST
FOR YEARS

Caleb Warnock

CONTENTS

REASONS TO PLANT A FOOD FOREST

1   Little or no maintenance work or time required

2   Food security

3   Self-reliance

4   The grocery store goes on without me

5   Bless future generations

6   Little or no water needed (designed for your climate)

7   No weeding (if desired)

8   No chemicals

9   Secret garden (few people would even recognize it as food)

10 Unpredictable temperatures and weather = no problem

11 Four-season eating

12 Shareable

13 Permaculture is sustainable and self-sufficient

WELCOME TO THE GARDEN OF EDEN!

A food forest is simply a place where Mother Nature can grow a garden for you with little or no human intervention. You plant the garden and leave it to "go wild," meaning that you permanently leave the care of the garden in the hands of Mother Nature.

In most climates, a food forest is never watered. Instead, the vegetables in the food forest rely entirely on whatever water nature provides. Even in dry climates, you can design a garden that never needs water or a garden that will be watered only during the summer. Unlike most backyard gardens, a food forest is created to be permanent and wild. Wild means you plant the garden once. There is no yearly planting. After the first year, a food forest should perpetuate itself.

MUST-HAVES: FOUR THINGS AND THREE DECISIONS

There are four things that you must have before you can start your food forest.

1. **Heirloom seeds and bulbs.** A food forest will survive long term only with true seeds, which are seeds and bulbs that are genetically stable. Hybrid and genetically modified seeds and bulbs are not genetically stable, meaning the seed of the plant will not produce true and may not produce at all in future generations.

2. **Heirloom live plants**, for the same reason listed above.

3. **Property.** If you don't own property, see the section of this book on borrowing a food forest or the section on creating a food forest on public land.

4. **Water** (optional) or **a knowledge of which plants don't need summer water in dry climates**.

Also, there are three decisions that you need to make before you can get started.

1. Determine who will know the location of the food forest and be allowed to harvest.

2. Determine to harvest only sustainably. If too much is harvested, the forest will disappear in a year or two (more on this later).

3. Do you want to control the weeds?

DESIGNING YOUR FOOD FOREST

The first step in designing your food forest is to consider your goals carefully. The worksheet below is designed to help you pinpoint your harvest goals. DO NOT plan to fill out the worksheet now. Instead, read the worksheet as an overview of some of the questions you will need to consider as you read this book. When you've read all the information you need, come back to the worksheet to help you start putting your plan in action.

1   My food forest location is (circle one):
    A   land I plan to own long term
    B   land I plan to own for only a few years
    C   public land with public access and permission
          from the proper authority in writing

D   wild land without written permission

Ɛ   land someone else owns (borrowed land)

2   The estimated size of my food forest is _____ square feet. (To find this measurement, multiply the length by the width of the garden space you plan to have.)

3   Garden map: create a rough sketch of your garden space, showing your home (if your food forest will be near your home).

4   Direct sun? Label areas of the garden that are in full shade, part shade, or dappled light.

5   My food forest will be (circle):

A   dry in summer

B   watered in summer (rain or sprinkler)

6   My food forest will include (circle all that apply):

A   root vegetables

B   salad greens

C   grains

D   potherbs

E   flowers for beauty

f   culinary herbs

8   medicinal herbs

H   outdoor seating or living area

i   decorative fountain or water feature

J   invasives in pots

K   invasives in the soil

L   grape vine(s): purple, rose, white champagne

7. Berry bushes (circle all that apply):

A   raspberries

B   blackberries

C   boysenberries

D   blueberries

E   currants

f   goji

8   nanking cherry bush

H   other

i   none

8. Fruit trees (circle all that apply):

A   apple

B   pear

C   peach

D   apricot

E   plum

f   hardy kiwi

8   nectarine

H   cherry

i   figs

J   nut trees

K   tropicals

L   other

M   none

Favorites. List your must-haves here:

10   Choose one. All dollar amounts below are equivalent to the prices you would pay to buy the same organic food:

A   I need my food forest to be small, producing $100 to $500 worth of fresh produce annually

B   Medium harvest of $1,000 to $2,000 worth of fresh produce annually

C   Large self-reliant harvest that will provide the majority of my family's food

11   What is the rough budget for creating my food forest? (The budget should cover the cost of seeds, bulbs, and live plants, as well as design and installation, if needed.)

12   The vegetable portion of the garden will be (circle one):

A   Mostly root vegetables (self-reliance)

B   Mostly greens (salad garden)

BEST VEGETABLES FOR FOOD FORESTS

ASPARAGUS

Harvestable in: spring
Summer water (dry climate): not needed
Natural propagation: multiplier bulbs/roots
Spreading? creeping
Sun requirements: full sun, full shade, part shade

BELGIAN WINTER LEEKS

Harvestable in: spring, summer, autumn, winter, storage
Summer water (dry climate): occasional (every 2–3 weeks)
Natural propagation: self-seeding, multiplier bulbs/ roots
Spreading? creeping
Sun requirements: full sun, full shade, part shade

NOTE: ALSO PRODUCES ELEPHANT GARLIC BULBS, WHICH WILL MULTIPLY.

BLACKBERRIES

Harvestable in: summer, autumn
Summer water (dry climate): occasional (every 2–3 weeks)
Natural propagation: perennial

Spreading? not in dry climates; invasive in wet climates
Sun requirements: full sun, full shade, part shade

BROAD WINDSOR FAVA BEAN

Harvestable in: summer, storage
Summer water (dry climate): not needed
Natural propagation: self-seeding
Spreading? no
Sun requirements: full sun, part shade

BROOM CORN

Harvestable in: autumn, storage
Summer water (dry climate): occasional (every 2 weeks)
Natural propagation: self-seeding
Spreading? no
Sun requirements: full sun

NOTE: BROOM CORN DOES NOT FORM COBS LIKE GARDEN CORN, BUT IT IS EDIBLE. BROOM CORN IS A FORM OF CORN THAT MORE CLOSELY RESEMBLES CORN IN NATURE (WILD CORN, ALSO CALLED LANDRACE CORN), AND THIS IS WHY IT MAY BE POSSIBLE TO GROW IT IN A FOOD FOREST. YOU SHOULD PLANT 100 BROOM CORN SEEDS AT THE VERY MINIMUM, AND 250 FOR BETTER LONG-TERM SUCCESS. YOU WILL NEED TO ALLOW BETWEEN 100 AND 200 SEEDS TO FALL TO THE GROUND EACH YEAR TO SELF-PLANT, SO KEEP THIS IN MIND WHEN HARVESTING BROOM CORN FROM A FOOD FOREST.

BUCKWHEAT

Harvestable in: summer, autumn, storage

Summer water (dry climate): occasional (every 2–3
weeks)

Natural propagation: self-seeding

Spreading? creeping

Sun requirements: full sun, part shade

CHICKWEED

Harvestable in: spring, summer, autumn, storage
(blanch & freeze)

Summer water (dry climate): occasional (every 2–3
weeks)

Natural propagation: self-seeding

Spreading? invasive

Sun requirements: full sun, full shade, part shade

CHIVES

Harvestable in: spring, summer, (early) autumn

Summer water (dry climate): occasional (every 2–3
weeks)

Natural propagation: self-seeding, multiplier bulbs/
roots, perennial

Spreading? no

Sun requirements: full sun, full shade, part shade

COLLARD GREENS, VATES

Harvestable in: spring, summer, autumn, winter

Summer water (dry climate): occasional (every 2–3 weeks)

Natural propagation: self-seeding

Spreading? creeping

Sun requirements: full sun, full shade, part shade

CURRANTS

Harvestable in: summer

Summer water (dry climate): occasional (every 2–3 weeks)

Natural propagation: perennial

Spreading? creeping

Sun requirements: full sun, full shade, part shade

DEEP WINTER LETTUCE

Harvestable in: spring, summer, autumn

Summer water (dry climate): weekly

Natural propagation: self-seeding

Spreading? creeping

Sun requirements: full sun, full shade, part shade

DWARF BLUE SIBERIAN KALE

Harvestable in: spring, autumn, early winter

Summer water (dry climate): not needed

Natural propagation: self-seeding

Spreading? creeping
Sun requirements: full sun, full shade, part shade

EGYPTIAN WALKING ONIONS

Harvestable in: spring (bottom), summer (top), autumn
(top), storage
Summer water (dry climate): not needed
Natural propagation: multiplier bulbs/roots
Spreading? creeping
Sun requirements: full sun, full shade, part shade

ELEPHANT GARLIC

(see Belgian winter leeks)

GARLIC

Harvestable in: summer, autumn, storage
Summer water (dry climate): occasional (every 2–3
weeks)
Natural propagation: multiplier bulb
Spreading? no
Sun requirements: full sun, part shade

GARLIC CHIVES

Harvestable in: spring, summer, (early) autumn
Summer water (dry climate): occasional (every 2–3
weeks)

Natural propagation: self-seeding, multiplier bulbs/
    roots, perennial
Spreading? creeping
Sun requirements: full sun, full shade, part shade

GOJI BERRY

Harvestable in: summer, autumn
Summer water (dry climate): occasional (every 2–3
    weeks)
Natural propagation: perennial
Spreading? creeping
Sun requirements: full sun, full shade, part shade

GREEN MOUNTAIN MULTIPLIER HUGE ONIONS

Harvestable in: summer, autumn, storage
Summer water (dry climate): occasional (every 2–3
    weeks)
Natural propagation: multiplier bulbs/roots
Spreading? creeping
Sun requirements: full sun

HORSERADISH

Harvestable in: spring, summer, autumn, winter, storage
Summer water (dry climate): occasional (every 2–3
    weeks)
Natural propagation: multiplier bulbs/roots
Spreading? invasive
Sun requirements: full sun, full shade, part shade

INDIAN WOMAN YELLOW BUSH BEAN

Harvestable in: summer, storage

Summer water (dry climate): weekly until dead in midsummer

Natural propagation: self-seeding

Spreading? no

Sun requirements: full sun, part shade

LEMON BALM

Harvestable in: spring, summer, autumn, storage

Summer water (dry climate): occasional (every 2–3 weeks)

Natural propagation: self-seeding, perennial

Spreading? creeping

Sun requirements: full sun, full shade, part shade

OATS

Harvestable in: summer, autumn, storage

Summer water (dry climate): occasional (every 2–3 weeks)

Natural propagation: self-seeding

Spreading? creeping

Sun requirements: full sun, part shade

OREGANO

Harvestable in: spring, summer, autumn, storage

Summer water (dry climate): occasional (every 2–3 weeks)

Natural propagation: self-seeding, perennial
Spreading? invasive
Sun requirements: full sun, full shade, part shade

PARSLEY

Harvestable in: spring, summer, storage
Summer water (dry climate): occasional (every 2–3
    weeks)
Natural propagation: self-seeding
Spreading? creeping
Sun requirements: full sun, full shade, part shade

PARSNIPS

Harvestable in: autumn, winter, storage
Summer water (dry climate): not needed
Natural propagation: self-seeding
Spreading? no
Sun requirements: full sun, part shade

PEAS (CASCADIA, GOLDEN SWEET, JUMP)

Harvestable in: spring, summer, autumn, storage
    (freeze)
Summer water (dry climate): occasional (every 2–3
    weeks, especially in shade)
Natural propagation: self-seeding
Spreading? no
Sun requirements: full sun, full shade, part shade

RASPBERRIES

Harvestable in: summer

Summer water (dry climate): occasional (every 2–3 weeks)

Natural propagation: perennial

Spreading? creeping

Sun requirements: full sun, full shade, part shade

SALSIFY

Harvestable in: spring, autumn, winter, storage

Summer water (dry climate): not needed

Natural propagation: self-seeding

Spreading? creeping

Sun requirements: full sun, part shade

SHALLOTS

Harvestable in: summer, autumn, storage

Summer water (dry climate): occasional (every 2–3 weeks)

Natural propagation: multiplier bulbs/roots

Spreading? no

Sun requirements: full sun, part shade

STRAWBERRIES

Harvestable in: summer, autumn

Summer water (dry climate): occasional (every 2–3 weeks)

Natural propagation: perennial
Spreading? creeping
Sun requirements: full sun, full shade, part shade

SUMMER SAVORY

Harvestable in: summer, autumn, early winter, storage
Summer water (dry climate): occasional (every 2–3 weeks)
Natural propagation: perennial
Spreading? no
Sun requirements: full sun, full shade, part shade

SUNCHOKES

Harvestable in: spring, storage
Summer water (dry climate): occasional (every 2–3 weeks)
Natural propagation: multiplier bulbs/roots
Spreading? invasive
Sun requirements: full sun, part shade

SWISS CHARD

Harvestable in: spring, summer, autumn, early winter, storage (freeze)
Summer water (dry climate): occasional (every 2–3 weeks)
Natural propagation: self-seeding
Spreading? creeping
Sun requirements: full sun, full shade, part shade

TOMATOES, WINTER GRAPE

Harvestable in: summer, autumn, storage
Summer water (dry climate): weekly
Natural propagation: self-seeding
Spreading? no
Sun requirements: full sun

TURNIP (VARIETIES: PURPLE TOP, GOLD, VERTUS MARTEAU)

Harvestable in: summer, autumn, winter, storage
Summer water (dry climate): occasional (every 2–3 weeks)
Natural propagation: self-seeding
Spreading? no
Sun requirements: full sun, part shade

NOTE: WINTER HARVEST MAY NOT LAST ALL WINTER. WINTER-HARVESTED BULBS MAY NEED TO BE USED BEFORE THEY UNTHAW.

WILD SQUASH

Harvestable in: summer, autumn, storage
Summer water (dry climate): weekly
Natural propagation: self-seeding
Spreading? no
Sun requirements: full sun

NOTE: FIVE NON-CROSSING TYPES

WINTER FINE FETTLE GREENS

Harvestable in: spring, summer, autumn, winter
Summer water (dry climate): occasional (every 2–3 weeks)
Natural propagation: self-seeding
Spreading? creeping
Sun requirements: full sun, full shade, part shade

BEST FLOWERS & HERBS FOR FOOD FORESTS

The best flowers and herbs for your food forest include calendula, alyssum, snapdragons, columbines, marigolds, purple coneflower, black-eyed Susan, dame's rocket, St. John's wort, all reliable self-seeding flowers, perennial flowers like lavender, and soapwort. Their requirements are largely as follows:

Summer water (dry climate): ranges from occasional (every 2–3 weeks) to not needed
Natural propagation: self-seeding, perennial
Spreading? creeping
Sun requirements: ranges; full sun, full shade, part shade

CULINARY AND MEDICINAL HERBS

Summer water (dry climate): occasional (every 2–3 weeks)

Natural propagation: self-seeding, perennial

Spreading? creeping

Sun requirements: ranges; full sun, full shade, part shade

CULINARY HERBS FOR FOOD FORESTS

Fennel (creeping to invasive)

Oregano (invasive)

Thyme (creeping)

Winter savory (bush)

Summer savory (bush)

Dill (creeping)

Marjoram (invasive)

Sage (bush)

Spearmint (invasive)

Peppermint (invasive)

MEDICINAL HERBS FOR FOOD FORESTS

Elecampane (yellow sunflower type)

Horehound (white bush flowers)

Hyssop (purple spike flower)

Lemon balm

Catnip (purple spike flower)

Motherwort (tall purple spike flower)

St. John's wort (yellow bush flower)

Calendula (orange daisy-type flower)
Feverfew (tiny white-and-yellow daisy-type flower)
German chamomile (tiny white-and-yellow daisy-type
    flower)
Comfrey (invasive)
Yarrow (creeping)

WILD EDIBLES FOR FOOD FORESTS

Wild edibles are what most people call "weeds," but some of the things that we think are a bother are actually great sources of tasty, free food. This list includes not just greens, but also grains, root vegetables, and protein-rich seeds. If some of these grow naturally in your area, you may want to strongly consider transplanting some of them into your food forest area. There are several benefits to planting these "weeds" instead of just looking for them in the wild or hoping they grow on your property, including:

- You will always have legal access to them if they are on your property.

- You will be able to study their lifecycles more closely. This will allow you to better know the best times to harvest these wild edibles.

- You can be sure the plants are clean. One of the dangers of harvesting from the wild is that if you gather from a roadside, the plants are likely coated with fine particles of car exhaust. If you gather from wild lands, you don't know if the plants have been walked on (or worse) by wild animals.

- Most importantly, if you plant wild edibles with seeds from a guaranteed source, such as SeedRenaissance.com, then you don't have to guess that you have correctly identified a wild plant. Most wild plants have look-alikes that can be dangerous or even poisonous, so you should never ever wildcraft (gather from the wild) any plant for eating unless you are with an expert or have expert-level experience. Looking at pictures online and then trying to gather wild food is dangerous because what the Internet may not show you is all the plants that look similar to the wild plant you are hunting. Use wisdom and caution when wildcrafting.

  - Blue mustard (*Chorispora tenella*) leaves
  - Black medick (*Medicago lupulina*) leaves and seeds, cooked
  - Cereal rye (*Secale cereale*) grain
  - Chickweed (*Stellaria media*) leaves and seeds, raw or cooked (invasive; seeds 18% protein, 6% fat)

- Common dandelion (*Taraxacum officinale*) flowers, leaves, and roots, raw or cooked
- Common mallow (*Malva neglecta*) leaves and seeds, raw or cooked
- Common purslane (*Portulaca oleracea*) leaves and stems, raw or cooked
- Flixweed (*Descurainia sophia*) leaves and seeds (seeds 25% protein, 26% fat)
- Henbit (*Lamium amplexicaule*) leaves, raw or cooked
- Kochia (*Kochia scoparia*) leaves and seeds (seeds 20% protein, 8% fat) *Note: kochia pollen is a common allergen*
- Plains prickly pear cactus (*Opuntia polyacantha*) seeds, fruit, pad (beware thorns)
- Purple dead-nettle (*Lamium purpureum*) leaves, raw or cooked
- Redroot pigweed (*Amaranthus retroflexus*) leaves and seeds, raw or cooked
- Redstem filaree (*Erodium cicutarium*)
- Shepherd's purse (*Capsella bursa-pastoris*) leaves, flowers, roots, and seeds, raw or cooked (leaves 3% protein and rich in iron, calcium, and vitamin C; seeds 35% oil)
- Venice mallow (*Hibiscus trionum*) leaves, raw or cooked

- Yellow salsify (*Tragopogon dubius*) root and leaves, raw or cooked

FOR MORE INFORMATION ON ANY OF THESE WILD EDIBLES, TO CHECK WHETHER SPECIFIC PLANTS ARE EDIBLE, OR TO SEE CERTAIN CAUTIONS ABOUT EDIBLE PLANTS, YOU CAN RESEARCH INDIVIDUAL PLANTS BY COMMON NAME OR SCIENTIFIC NAME AT PFAF.ORG.

WHAT NOT TO PLANT

If all vegetables thrived in a food forest situation, then vegetables would be weeds. Imagine that kind of world! Unfortunately, that is science fiction. For reasons beyond the scope of this book, the following vegetables will not survive from year to year in most food forests.

- Basil
- Brassicas, including broccoli, cauliflower, kale, Asian greens, and many more
- Beets
- Cantaloupes
- Carrots
- Celery

- Corn

- Cucumbers

- Eggplant

- Garden squash (cultivar squash)

- Lemongrass

- Potatoes

- Radishes

- Peppers

- Watermelons and all garden melons

GENERAL SUN REQUIREMENTS

These are basic requirements for the different types of plants to consider as you lay out your food forest.

> Lettuce, salad greens, and herbs tolerate full sun, part shade, and full shade. The more sun they get, however, the faster and larger they will grow.

> Fruiting vegetable plants (tomatoes, squash, corn, melons, etc.) flourish in full sun only.

> Root and bulb vegetables must have at least a quarter day of sun. This means at least six hours of direct sunlight per day.

POTHERBS (POTTAGE PLANTS)

I know, I know; I've heard the jokes many times. But this is NOT a section about marijuana. Historically, potherbs were the fast food of everyday life before the invention of the grocery store. Potherbs are any greens that can be quickly taken from the garden or surrounding landscape and cooked for a quick meal, typically lunch. The 1828 edition of *Webster's Dictionary* defines potherbs as "an herb for the pot or for cookery; a culinary plant." Potherbs are basically any edible plant with food value. These include beet greens, collards, kale, mustard leaf, turnip greens, spinach, and swiss chard.

We know from documented history that potherbs have been a staple food for thousands of years. They were eaten raw, boiled, steamed, or sautéed. Grains were added when available. Probably the most common use for potherbs was pottage, a soup or stew that was eaten immediately or left on the edge of the fire to keep warm for days so that it could be eaten as needed. Sometimes, additional water and ingredients were added (as wanted) to the existing soup. Meat was added if you had the money or were able to catch something from the wild. Potherbs and pottage have been used in many different cultures throughout time. Potherbs were also used to stuff pasta. To this day, people in parts of Italy make a dish called *preboggion*, which uses wild greens to stuff ravioli. This is a dish I make on occasion. Wild greens are also used in Italy today to add to egg dishes like frittata and, of course, in soups like minestrone.

Whether an edible weed is a weed or a food is a matter of perspective. Corey Eilhardt, on the Cloisters Museum and Gardens website, wrote that "a weed is a plant you don't want. An herb is a plant with a use. But many of the 'weedy' species that are considered garden nuisances today were actually valued in the Middle Ages." He continues by explaining that "edible weeds growing in the kitchen garden, along with the cultivated vegetables, were used in pottage, a basic medieval dish. Although medieval gardeners took means to eliminate weeds within field crops like wheat, when they dug up cabbages and leeks, they also harvested the edible weeds growing nearby and boiled everything together in the same pot."

For modern homesteaders—or anyone who wants to be more self-reliant and healthy—potherbs are invaluable. Many of the food forest plants recommended in this book can be used as potherbs or for pottage.

HOW TO START A PUBLIC FOOD FOREST

public food forest can help any community, and it just needs an instigator: you! When you propose a public food forest, however, you should recognize that this becomes a community project and is more successful if you go through the correct channels to organize supplies, efforts, and education. These steps can help you get started.

STEP 1. Identify the exact area in a public park or public open space that you believe would be the ideal space for a public food forest.

STEP 2. Create a detailed list of what you would plant, who would donate which specific plants, bulbs, and seeds, and who would install the food forest (plant it). Be clear that any member of the public may harvest the food forest. Ask if it is possible to put information in a city newsletter or website explaining how not to overharvest the food forest so it can continue long term.

STEP 3. Make a list of examples of successful local food forests and a few national examples that are aspirational.

STEP 4. Create a written document explaining what a food forest is, why it would benefit the public, why it should be on public land, and all information from Steps 1, 2, and 3.

STEP 5. Approach an elected official (city council member, for example), briefly explain what you want and why you want it, and give them a copy of your written document. Ask them if they would be willing to help promote your proposal. Set up an appointment to get back with them to discuss your proposal after they have had time to look over the written document. Check back in person or email. Don't be tempted to skip this step and go straight to the council or authority without a sponsor. You are more likely to fail without a sponsor.

STEP 6. If the elected official is supportive, work with them to get your proposal on a specific meeting agenda.

STEP 7. Once your proposal is scheduled for a meeting, prepare a five- to ten-minute presentation to give an explanation of your proposal in the meeting. Use pictures if possible. Be clear and concise and focus on the public benefits of your proposal. Be sure to explain that the city would not need to spend any money, devote any staff time, or change any existing property use. Explain that the food forest can be removed if needed. Be logical and convincing. Don't be emotional or uninformed.

Good luck! If you do propose a public food forest, I may be able to offer help or seed donations. Contact me at caleb-warnock@yahoo.com. Please remember that you must have my permission to use any part of this book in your proposal or presentation.

HOW TO BORROW A FOOD FOREST

I f you don't have property to put a food forest on and getting permission for a public food forest is not working, ask a neighbor or elderly couple or anyone with an unused garden space if you can install a food forest on their land. Explain that you would install the food forest and share the harvest with the property owner. Here are some guidelines to keep in mind.

- Be sure to get specific permission before installing anything invasive or permanent, like fruit trees or berry bushes.

- Be clear about whether you have the right to remove plants, bushes, etc., if the land owner changes their mind.

- Be clear about how you will share the harvest. Will it be a 50/50 split? Will you alert the property owner when certain things are ready to harvest? Will you harvest it for them and leave a portion on their doorstep?

- Be clear about how and when you have permission to access the property—which gate to use, for example. Leave all gates the way you found them.

- Never leave the property with the water running. Be clear whether you are going to contribute financially toward the cost of water and how often you would use the water.

THE CLEAN AND TIDY FOOD FOREST

To weed or not to weed? Most true food forests are left in their wild state, but depending on where the forest is located, this may or may not work. If you are using part of your lawn, you need to think carefully about whether you will weed the food forest occasionally. Here are some options for keeping control of the weeds in your food forest.

1   Spot-spray with my edible weedkiller spray, available at SeedRenaissance.com.

2   Spot-kill with my edible weedkiller recipe, which is applied with a paintbrush or paint roller, not sprayed on. Recipe for sale at SeedRenaissance.com.

3   Use concentrated vinegar (glacial acetic acid) that has been diluted to 10 to 20 percent and spot-spray with this dilution.

4   Weed occasionally by hand, especially in late spring and early summer. The goal of occasional weeding is to keep the weeds from producing seeds. If you allow the weeds to produce seeds, you are in a losing battle. But if you weed enough to keep the weeds from producing seeds, over the years, your food forest will naturally become less and less weedy.

5   Weed by hand religiously to keep weeds removed.

If you don't control the weeds, the food forest may be unsightly, prompting complaints from neighbors. Garden pests (slugs, snails, etc.) will also multiply. The weeds, which are naturally aggressive, will certainly shade out some of your vegetables and steal nutrients and water from them. This will mean a smaller harvest for you and, over time, some vegetables will die out.

SUSTAINABLE HARVESTING

When they have gone to seed, most food plants are totally unrecognizable. For example, a head of lettuce will become six feet tall and produce long stems of small yellow or white flowers. The plant will no longer look like a head of lettuce at all. If you do weed, be sure not to remove the vegetables that have gone to seed. Seeds must be allowed to develop, mature, and dry naturally in the food forest. This will have a weedy appearance in spring, summer, or autumn, depending on the vegetable. If you remove the vegetables that have gone to seed, those vegetables will not appear in your food forest again, and you will have to replant or reseed.

Everything in the food forest must reproduce from year

to year or the food forest will cease to exist. Here are some guidelines:

- Self-seeding plants should be harvested only partially. Allow at least ten plants from each vegetable type to go to seed each year. After seed is produced, many vegetable plants, but not all, die. Allow the seed to fully dry and naturally drop to the ground before you attempt to remove any of the dead plant debris. For more information about how to save true vegetable seeds, click on "Classes" at SeedRenaissance.com or, if the class is not listed at the website, contact calebwarnock@yahoo.com.

- Plants that reproduce by multiplying bulbs or roots must be carefully harvested so that at least one bulb, rhizome, or root remains from each plant. For example, if you are growing multiplier onions, you will plant one onion bulb, and next year, that one bulb will have multiplied to become a dozen or more onion bulbs. When you harvest this clump of bulbs, leave the largest bulb. If you accidentally pull this one up, replant it immediately. The rest of the bulbs in the clump may be harvested for eating.

- Plants that are perennial will either never die (at least not for many years) or will die back in the winter and grow anew each spring. But if you overharvest these plants, it may kill them. Summer savory, for example, is one of my most used culinary herbs. In the garden, it is a small perennial bush. But harvesting more than two-thirds of the leaves could kill the plant. As a general rule of thumb, never harvest more than two-thirds of any perennial plant.

REVERSE SEASONS IN A FOOD FOREST

A typical summer garden is planted in spring or early summer and is harvested in autumn. A food forest, however, is not a typical garden. Food forests use only vegetables and herbs that are perennial (live for many years) or are reliable self-seeders, meaning they produce enough true seed each year to grow an equal or greater number of plants than the previous year. Most typical garden plants are not perennial or reliable self-seeders. (If they were, vegetables would grow like weeds!) Perennials and self-seeders are best planted in autumn. Perennials and self-seeders are healthiest and strongest if they are allowed to become established in cool temperatures. Some seeds must be exposed to a winter's worth of freezing temperatures or they will not germinate in spring. This odd timing also exposes the young plant to the winter solstice, which is critical for seed production in many plants.

WHY ORDER FROM SEEDRENAISSANCE.COM?

- First, I literally search the globe for the last seeds of important historic varieties, like perennial wheat. I am singlehandedly keeping alive many critical heirloom varieties. You can read about this in my book *Forgotten Skills of Self-Sufficiency Used by the Mormon Pioneers*. (Learn more at CalebWarnock.blogspot.com.)

- Second, for every common heirloom I offer, I've grown and rejected thirty to forty other varieties. I spend huge time and money on these tests, because no one else is doing this work. I evaluate how these varieties perform in an organic garden without petrochemical fertilizer, pesticides, or herbicides. I evaluate earliness, flavor, production, storage, cold soil tolerance, winter harvest ability, self-seeding capacity, and more. If I don't love a variety, I don't sell it.

- Finally, every seed I sell is guaranteed pure and NEVER hybrid, GMO, patented, or corporate owned. Our food supply MUST remain in the public domain. Join me in creating a renaissance in our backyard gardens.

FOOD FORESTS & EDIBLE PARKS

- Eagle Mountain, Utah (designed and planted by me)
- Pleasant Grove, Utah (designed and planted by me)
- Fruita, Utah (Capitol Reef National Park; planted by pioneers)
- Basalt Food Park, Colorado
- Philadelphia Orchard project, Pennsylvania (54 orchards today)
- Collingwood Food Forest, Toledo, Ohio
- Rahma Edible Forest Snack Garden, Syracuse, New York
- Spring Ridge Commons (Canada's oldest)

QUESTIONS AND ANSWERS

Question: How do I design a food forest that can be maintained for many years without any human intervention?

Answer: Plant only those vegetables that are listed in this book as not needing water in summer.

Q: How do I design a food forest that can be maintained for many years with only limited human intervention?

A: Plant only those vegetables that are listed in this book as needing only occasional water in summer or not needing water in summer. Remember that plants requiring occasional water will die without water every two or three weeks.

They may also produce less than plants watered weekly, so be prepared for potentially smaller harvests. In years of extreme or above average temperatures, a food forest may need more than occasional water, especially those parts exposed to full sun.

Q: Do I have to water a lot in the beginning to get the food forest established?

A: Not if you plant in autumn, as explained in the "Reverse Seasons" chapter of this book.

Q: What is the best resource for purchasing heirloom berries, currants, and fruit trees for my food forest?

A: Costco has the best fruit trees each spring, about $10 each. Berries and currants you can get for free from local gardeners.

Q: You said not to plant any brassicas in the food forest, but you have listed Vates collard greens as one of the recommended vegetables. What gives?

A: Vegetables of the species *Brassica oleracea* (collards, broccoli, kale, cabbage, kohlrabi, brussels sprouts) basically revert to collard greens overtime. Collard greens are pretty close to the wild state of this species, and this is why this vegetable is not only acceptable in our food forest, but also a great potherb that has been used for centuries, especially in the hunger gap.

Q: Can I plant a food forest on a steep slope?

A: Yes. The slope may have some limitations because slopes drain faster than level ground, but many things will grow on a slope.

Q: Can I plant a food forest on my lawn without removing the grass?

A: No. The seeds need direct access to the soil. You can plant trees and bushes in grass, however.

Q: My spouse is reluctant to let me plant a food forest. Any advice?

A: Spousal approval is overrated. And if you plant the right things, they may never even know you have planted the food forest because it will blend into the weeds! If nothing else, start small with plants that your spouse will enjoy.

Q: How soon after I plant my food forest will it be established enough for me to harvest?

A: Good question. You will need to wait a year before you begin to harvest, long enough that the seeds you plant have grown and thrown seeds of their own to the ground.

Q: Can a permaculture food forest be decorative? Does it have to be "wild"?

A: The food forest can be as decorative as you want, but remember that many vegetables may look "weedy" when they are producing seed.

Q: If there is a dry spell, can I water my food forest by hand or must I install a sprinkler system (if I have chosen to have the kind of food forest that is watered occasionally in dry climates)?

A: Watering by hand is fine.

Q: You have suggested that I decide whether to plant a food forest that will entirely take care of itself without any intervention or watering by me or a food forest that is occasionally watered if I live in a dry climate. Can I have both? Can I plant everything I want, and water occasionally, and then if for some reason I don't have access to water, let the food forest plants that need occasional water die, leaving just the drought-tolerant plants?

A: Whew! That question was a mouthful! The answer is yes. You can plant everything I have recommended and then let the things that need water die if water becomes unavailable. Keep in mind, however, that some of the plants that I have listed in this book as never needing water may appear to be dead in the heat of summer only to reappear the next spring. These plants are dormant, not dead.

Q: Don't gardens have to be rotated for health? Do I need to rotate my food forest crops?

A: Mother Nature will rotate the crops for you. They will slowly move around from year to year as they throw their seeds and multiply their bulbs. You don't need to worry about rotating.

Q: How much property must I have for a food forest?

A: Good question. A food forest can be quite small or quite large. The size of the food forest is entirely up to you.

Q: How many seeds need to fall to the ground?

A: This is a complex question, based on genetics, and the answer may surprise you. The number of plants that throw seed is actually more important than the total number of seeds. For best genetic health, most vegetables need at least ten plants to produce seeds each year in a food forest. This will produce more seed than you need, but keep in mind that birds and other animals are also going to harvest your food forest, so having too much seed is not a big problem. (However, if you see certain plants from your food forest, like vernal red orach, trying to spread aggressively beyond your planned food forest area, you may want to collect some of the seeds instead of letting them fall.) Spinach is a rare exception in the garden world and, without going into genetic detail, let me just suggest that a minimum of twenty spinach plants should be allowed to go to seed each year in your food forest. The good news is that you can harvest the outer leaves of each spinach plant without damaging its ability to produce seed.

Q: If I grow hybrid squash in my garden and insects cross-pollinate this with the heirloom squash in my food forest, will this mean my food forest squash might eventually die out (because hybrid pollination is often unstable)? Can I grow both vining and bush squashes in the food forest? Will they cross?

A: Squash cross up to a half-mile, and if you grow hybrid squash in your garden, they will certainly cross with the heirlooms in the food forest. This can indeed cause, over the course of several years, your heirloom squashes to die out, and it will certainly guarantee that your "wild" squash will indeed be wild and extremely unpredictable because of the hybrid pollen. I don't believe in growing, selling, or using hybrid seeds for this and other reasons. You can read more about this in my first book, *Forgotten Skills of Self-Sufficiency Used by the Mormon Pioneers*. For now, you can choose to buy seeds only from me, at my website, SeedRenaissance.com, because I sell only pure heirloom seeds.

Q: Do some of the plants recommended by you grow as weeds, meaning they might spread?

A: Some of them are considered weeds and may spread if you don't harvest them. The goal of a food forest is to provide food. If you plant the food forest and never harvest any food from it, not only is the effort a failure, but the things you have planted may spread beyond the space you designated for your "forest" as they multiply from year to year. To avoid this, harvest these plants.

Q: Can I grow my food forest and my regular vegetable garden side by side?

A: Yes. Some crossing will happen, but some crossing is likely to happen in the food forest anyway because many vegetables can cross with any similar species a half mile. Long story short: don't worry about crossing, because you cannot control it.

Q: Online and in other places, there is a lot of evidence placed on "layering" the food forest by growing certain things under certain other things. I notice you have not talked about this at all. Why?

A: Layering is kind of a gimmick. I have listed in this book which food forest plants need full sun and which don't. Those that don't can be planted in shade if need be, but most plants prefer more sun than less (there are some exceptions). If you follow the guidelines in this book, you can design your food forest with or without layering. Obviously, if you have only a tiny space for your food forest, or if you are trying to maximize your existing space, then layering is a good idea. Just make sure you plant the vegetables that need full sun in the right places and those that can tolerate partial shade in the right places; keep in mind that the number of vegetables that can tolerate total shade is small.

Q: Help! I had *X* vegetable in my food forest, but now, after several years, it is gone! What happened? What do I do about it?

A: For genetic reasons that are beyond the scope of this book, some vegetables may slowly disappear from a food forest. Ideally, several dozen plants of each vegetable type should be allowed to go to seed in the food forest each year. And then, the next year, there would need to be at least as many babies that live to maturity as died the year before. In other words, the food forest would have to produce twenty swiss chard plants each year in order for swiss chard to be genetically stable enough to continue long term in the garden (although, over decades, twenty plants would not be enough). When the population of sexually reproducing plants falls below certain levels, those gene pools are too small and the entire population of that species dies out in that area. This is a very short explanation of a very long and technical truth. Suffice it to say that occasionally your food forest may need to be rejuvenated with new seeds, bulbs, or live plants. Tomatoes and wild squash may be especially in need of occasional replanting. It is also CRITICAL that you plant only the varieties list in this book. For example, I have listed a couple of kinds of onions. Don't be fooled into thinking that this means you can plant any onion—you can't. Most onion varieties won't survive more than a year or two in a food forest, for genetic and cultivar reasons that are beyond the scope of this book. I have spent years determining which vegetable types work best in a food forest situation. Also, keep in mind that there are many natural or uncontrollable ways for entire crops to fail. Erratic weather; pest infestations; drought; flood; soil disease; leaf disease; pollution of the air, water, or soil—all of these could cause a particular vegetable variety to fail in the food forest. But over time, genetic issues are likely to be the top threat of your food forest, which is why it is critical that you plant only the varieties I have listed here. Science calls some of these varieties "landrace," which, simply put, means they are most stable in the wild, where pollination is not controlled by isolation.

ABOUT THE AUTHOR

Caleb Warnock lives on the bench of the Rocky Mountains with his wife and family. He enjoys gardening and draws and paints when he is not writing, teaching, packing and shipping seeds, or creating new recipes. Caleb is the winner of more than twenty awards for writing and has a bachelor's degree in writing from Brigham Young University and a master's in writing from Utah State University. He is a certified nutrition specialist. He can be found on Facebook. He sells pure—never GMO, never hybrid—vegetable seeds at SeedRenaissance.com. He is the best-selling author of twenty nonfiction books and a novel with recipes, including:

The Art of Baking with Natural Yeast (coauthored by Melissa Richardson): Most people don't know that yeast in the grocery store has been modified in a laboratory to the point that it no longer digests the gluten naturally found in wheat. Natural yeast (also called sourdough, although it doesn't have to be sour) acts to prevent gluten intolerance, does not spike the glycemic index, controls allergies, and prevents heartburn.

Backyard Winter Gardening: Growing fresh winter vegetables is what fed our ancestors for centuries before the invention of the modern grocery store. This is the first vegetable-by-vegetable guide to fresh winter gardening published in the United States and includes carrots, onions, cantaloupe, beans, peas, lettuce, greens, and much more.

The Forgotten Skills of Self-Sufficiency Used by the Mormon Pioneers: Learn about backyard seed saving, the pioneer vegetable seed bank, baking with natural yeast, cellaring without a root cellar, organic raised bed gardening, heirloom fruit trees, perennial flower gardens, recipes, and more.

Trouble's on the Menu (coauthored by Betsy Schow): After her estranged husband's unexpected death, Hallie goes to Tippy Canoe, Montana, to wrap up his estate. Her arrival begins awkwardly as she runs over the town gossip during a snowstorm. Fortunately, the attractive—and single!—town mayor is willing to lend her a hand. But when life starts to spiral out of control, Hallie must decide whether he's worth sticking around for. Favorite recipe: hot snow chocolate!

More Forgotten Skills of Self-Sufficiency: Caleb is back with a new collection of skills to help your family gain independence and self-reliance. Learn about self-seeding vegetables, collecting water from rain and snow, finding wild vegetables for everyday eating, and even making your own laundry soap. If you liked the first *Forgotten Skills* book, then you will love these additional techniques for becoming truly self-sufficient.

Forgotten Skills of Backyard Herbal Healing and Family Health (coauthored by Kirsten Skirvin): Modern medicine can work wonders, but most of it has roots in the healing powers you can find in your own backyard. This informative book teaches you to harvest, dry, and store herbs that will keep you healthy. Discover how to use natural remedies safely so you can nurture your family's wellness without leaving home.

Make Your Own Cheese: If you want cheese that's better tasting than your best store-purchased Romano or Parmesan—for one-third the cost!—this book is for you. Caleb, a celebrated self-sufficiency master, teaches you how to make seven different cheeses that are delicious, inexpensive, and, most importantly, fun and easy to create.

Make Your Own Hard Lotion (coauthored by Amberlee Rynn): Today's liquid commercial lotions have more toxic chemicals than we want to admit. Homemade liquid lotions have a shelf life of only a couple of weeks. Hard lotion, however, is the solution for those interested in avoiding commercial products or lotions with short shelf lives and who want smooth, soft skin.

ABOUT FAMILIUS

VISIT OUR WEBSITE: WWW.FAMILIUS.COM

JOIN OUR FAMILY

There are lots of ways to connect with us! Subscribe to our newsletters at www.familius.com to receive uplifting daily inspiration, essays from our Pater Familius, a free ebook every month, and the first word on special discounts and Familius news.

GET BULK DISCOUNTS

If you feel a few friends and family might benefit from what you've read, let us know and we'll be happy to provide you with quantity discounts. Simply email us at orders@familius.com.

CONNECT

Facebook: www.facebook.com/paterfamilius
Twitter: @familiustalk, @paterfamilius1
Pinterest: www.pinterest.com/familius
Instagram: @familiustalk

The most important work you ever do will be within the walls of your own home.